A Game called Life

Author: Serafima Lachplese

GRATITUDE

I would like to say the biggest "Thank you" to Zilvinas and Diana Elvikei for their support and reliance. You are my heroes.

From the bottom of my heart,I would like to say a big "Thank you" to Rimants and Liana Brazdeikei who believed in me and in my family when we were not believing in ourselves.

Thank you to Prof. (Mrs) Juliet George Garrick who was very patient and professional in helping me with this book.

Thank you to my son Yanis for his support and care.Keep your dreams big!

Again, I want to say a big "Thank you" to my son Arnis for his big heart and love.

Finally, I want to say a big "Thank you"to my son Imants for his honesty and help and to my daughter Ellie for her wisdom and loving heart.

Stay positive and Happy.
Work hard and don't give up hope.
Be open to criticism and keep learning.
Surround yourself with happy,warm and genuine people.

 -Tena Des

Table of Contents

Escape Rooms Game Benefits You

- improves our critical thinking and problem solving skills
- develops team building skills and communication
- piques the senses
- increases communication and social ability
- contributes towards our daily amount of physical exercise
- increases our memory capacity and ability
- increases our level of happiness and satisfaction
- creates unique memories
- puts you in the creative mindset to work
- colleagues ,friends ,family members will get to know one another a lot better as they work together to escape the room and celebrate the sense of achievement that comes with a successful escape

Creative Mindset

It was a bright hot day on 1st August, 2016 when this secret place at Shepherds' Bush, London was first opened.

It is known as 'The mystery place'.

Last three years, I worked at a family business called Escape rooms.When my son Yanis opened the mystery place, people didn't know what the Escape rooms were.So many times we had to explain what they were . It is four years-now and we are still explaining to all the new people what it is.

By the way, what are Escape rooms?It is a life game in which you can come physically with your family, friends,colleagues and we actually lock you up in a room and you have 60 minutes to escape.Throughout this experience I am reminded of our life.

We have 60-75 years in our life but in a room you have only 60 minutes.If some of us live longer, it is a bonus .What are you doing during this time - 60 minutes or 60 years?

I saw how people who were very close to escaping from the room and who still had 10 minutes gave up. These ones were not confident in themselves and little obstacle kept them away from the goal.10 minutes or 10 years are enough time to succeed and to reach the goal.

I saw couples who came to our venue before they started the game argue with each other and they came with a negative attitude.But magic happened when everyone of them started to take responsibility,take action, started to respect and help others.Those teams-when they escaped-were so happy. They kissed each other and believed each other more, trusted more and respected more than they did before they entered the Escape rooms.

In Escape rooms, you can't really do it on your own. It is the same in real life.The more you help others,the more you enjoy your life.Your confidence and your belief grow.

ESCAPE ROOMS

In Escape Rooms if you do not solve one puzzle every 5 -10 minutes,you can't really succeed. It is very similar to what happens in our real life.If we do not grow, not opening new doors, we may not achieve our new dreams. Maybe you think:"Yes, but it is a very small achievement". I know for sure that a little step forward is better than no step.10 minutes a day reading a book is better than you not reading at all.100 meters race or 10 minutes exercise is better than no exercise at all.

As you read, remember:

Don't read to be big;

Read to be down to earth.

Don't read to be smart;

Read to be real.

Don't read to memorize;Read to realize.

Don't read a lot;Read just enough to keep yourself curious and hungry to learn more,to keep getting younger as you grow older.

2. We don't know what we don't know.Can I ask you something?When you see something the first time, do you have a feeling?

It may not be true -they are crazy.

We think so because we did not know but it is still possible.

I think earlier,it was a general belief that you can't swim if you don't have hands or legs but Nick Vujicic had no legs, no arms but he lived an incredible life and he swam very well.

I think he went through a lot of disappointments and pains but he reached his goals.

Of course, it is not easy for 60 minutes or 60 years to go there ...Where? ....

Do you know where you want to be?Did you write down a minimum of 100 dreams that you really want to achieve? Are you happy to start changing your habits? What habits need to be changed? What about the people around you?

Zilvinas Elvikei, the Executive diamond is a renowned personality.This person has huge influence in so many people's lives. He helps so many people to start thinking differently.And as a result of changing their thinking, they changed their lives.

Zilvinas always remind sus about time.We can't control time.

Teams at Escape Rooms who were inside the rooms for 60 minutes said it is the quickest hour in their lives. How old are you now?Have the last 10 years gone so quickly? The next 10 years are going to be quicker. Are you ready to live life to the full?Many of you would probably say, "Yes, but how?"

When the first time you do an escape room you may not be able to escape the room and fail miserably but you would have an absolute blast and you will become been hooked on it. So, you will really truly enjoy it. It will bring fun and energy to you.

It is really great bonding experience for friends and family. It is time when you are away from your film for an hour and you can really work towards a common goal and just enjoy each others company and have a few laughs and you will be able to brag to your friends about how smart you are. So, it is a really good time.

Benefits of Escape Room

Now the purpose of an escape room is to make all of those people work closely together, so no matter how smart you are individually there is no way you could get out of these rooms by yourself. So, it is really going to require that you rely on other people for information and their excellence and this pursuit of excellence for you to be successful and that is not a scary thing it may seem like but actually it is a fun activity that people do together.

These days you work side-by-side but you do not actually need to interact; it is a bowling, you can go axe throwing fights of things, you go to dinner but with an escape room you really have to be together and you know and the conversation and communication is critical. I is remaining me Network Marketing .

So, we see examples of all kinds of people coming in the room who are young, old and all different types but they all have to suddenly talk to each other and everyone's important in the room and suddenly there is someone who is really great at finding things and there are other people who are great at putting them together and together they make an awesome team.

In most escape rooms when you go in and have lockers and the purpose of the locker is to make sure that you do not have any technology when you go in and you are probably wondering why so most of the time you go and they say; *"could you lock up your phones"* and it is not because we do not want you taking pictures inside the room although we do not want you taking pictures inside the room but there is a reason. Everyone seems to want to Google everything and these rooms are really about you working together and in proximity; in a close proximity to one another and not working across a network but acutely using your brain. The idea behind an escape room is not how the fastest you are on your phone but the idea behind an escape room is how you can use your brain to figure stuff out because you would figure out eventually.

There might be a new state room where people are doing something in two different rooms because that is kind of how people work now; they work across them to the puzzle but that is not what we do in an escape room; what we want to do is put you in the same room and have you solve problems together, like a hand-to-hand combat. We have got smart phones that have given us the opportunity to not to have be so smart so we are kind of individually smart phones dumb people and it is the reality. Our kids, our youngsters do not know even the basic things to themselves. When we put them in escape rooms we see very clearly the things our kids do not know how to read, for instance, maps because we have Google Maps. So, when we have actual maps, people have absolutely no idea how to use them. Similarly, in your car, once you start using your navigation system you forget how to get to your Hans house because the navigation says turn left there. Well, we want you to actually realize that you need to turn and pay attention to the clues that are in front of you and not be guided and these are only few disadvantages of the technology. So, all the time at the escape room what we find is as soon as we take the phones away there is this look of panic on people's faces, especially teens. You know everybody comes before you get started and we are going to ask everybody to lock up your cell phone, smart phones, any type of technology and they lock it up and they go.

One of the greatest joys of taking away the technology is you will see people sit side by side and next to each other in the rooms and you will you hear them really working together. Because it should be like that that no matter how much technology we use. You are still going to need people and unfortunately we have lost the art and people's ability and willingness to sit down next to each other and actually work through something hand-in-hand because we hide behind the email, we hide behind text, although we do call someone on the phone but we are still far from each other. People would rather call you on the phone then talk to you when they are right next to you and that just sad.

Technology is great and we use technology in the rooms as part of the puzzles, in any business, Specialty Network Marketing.

The technology helps us to and provides us fabulous ways to create puzzles that are interesting and that people will find intriguing but it is not technologies; it is in the hands of the people who are participating and that is the distinction to make technology for the purpose of creating something .When we have some vision or ideas in our mind, we can having it in ours hands.

So, lock up your technology and come and play and be prepared to have to use your brain and do not let the lack of technology scare you.Don't let anybody scare you to succeed, to reach your goals ,your dreams.

 It is actually make it more fun and you would be surprised how engaged you become when you do overcomes your fear

Self-development through Escape Room

Nowadays everyone in the world wants to improve themselves and wants to grow themselves. The self-development is an important factor for our life and there are many ways that you can use to develop your selves and grow you inner selves. For the last few years another self-development method has been introduced and that is the escape room. First it started from the games then it becomes physical where you can go with your friends and family and play the escape room.

When you are in an escape room it is very important to understand that it's not a piece of cake. One cannot solve it and escape from without using his or her mind's best capability. You have to give your more than best and you can never escape it alone and on your own without the help of your friends your family and your team mates that you have chosen to go with in an escape room.

So, in order to be successful in Escape Rooms you don't need a sharp brain to find the clues and finally understand them and solve them. You need team or people who already have experience and of course time. The clock is always ticking and you have the limited time to use your best skills and understanding to escape successfully. Time is ticking, do you achieve in your life what you want achieve? If you have money and free time do you continue doing what you doing today?

The today's world is way too fast for anything slow everyone wants to be multi-purposeful and achieve many things in just one go. With the invention of the internet it is possible to learn explore and have fun at the same time. The internet had made the world a global village and that has made us competitive to become more better and better and hence, improve our self-development. So to become the best possible version of yourself and to maximize your potential with the globalization you need an outlet, a platform for your self-growth. Now the best way of improving yourself the best platform is none other than the escape room. The second way, from my opinion the best, it always people with experience .Who have 20-30-40 years of experience and they become mentors.

- **Attentiveness to every tiny detail:**

You need to be the hyper aware to every tiny bit of detail when you are working to escape the room. Your observation needs to be more keen than your normal. You have to look at your surroundings more closely and you have to pay attention to the things that you have already seen and because the rooms are so large or maybe so small then you have to remember everything presented their or that you have already used to touched because everything is important in an escape room. you cannot miss the even the smallest clue or things you food to where you left them or if you have something in your pocket because if you are not paying attention you would be out of time and out of luck and couldn't break the locks and escape the game.

So the more you train yourself for the little bit details and the more you observe the smaller other aspects of life then you will find that you are more keen and aware of your surroundings in your real life with a sharp brain and a good memory.

- **The Time limit:**

To escape the room the time limit is from 45 to 60 minutes and you have no idea of who fast an hour can pass. You have mysteries and puzzles to solve and find out the clues and all this can consume your entire time. And of course trial and error is not something that you can afford in escape rooms. So when you started do something you have to think why you are doing this and would you achieve anything from it. You cannot be distracted and waste time roaming uselessly.

So, In order to escape you need to consider your time limit and manage it well without wasting any moment. If you are regular to escape room than of course you will learn to avoid unnecessary. You will have streamlined focus when achieving just your goal when you learn to manage time. This trait will be useful in your life when you learned the value of your time and avoid errors towards your goal.

- **The Critical Thinking:**

The critical thinking is one of the important aspects of your life but unfortunately people don't know the value of it and throw this buzzword around the people without really knowing the actual meaning. So, critical thinking is something the escape room encapsulates perfectly. To find the clues and solve the mysteries you need to be able to think critically. In Critical thinking you are not supposed to over analyze to the point of inaction but you are supposed to look at your situation decisively and to think the best course of action and to take best decision for you situation. With the present information that is provided to you and that maybe very limited but still you have to solve the puzzles and to think and learn the use of items that are in front of you. You have to even think about the things that are hidden from your eyes. The problems that are given in the escape room's even computer cannot solve so it is important that you think critically. You can become better at critical thinking by forcing yourself to think enough to find a solution; you should be desperate enough to think. In order to do that you have to force yourself in unique situations that inspire you to think critically; you need challenging situation and escape room is the best platform for you because it will allow to exercise that exact part of your brain with real life threatening situation that stimulate pressure on you. Under pressure is the best way to practice critical thinking. Not some actually live or die situation but enough serious to put stress on you to arose that thinking. And again escape room just do that for you.

- **The Teamwork:**

The best thing about escape room is they are made for groups. Sometimes in a lot of rooms you are with your family members and you have to work with them, although, working with friends is also difficult when you are in pressure but with strangers you need a different kind of approach, mind set and skill. You need to learn to rely on other and trust them, understand them, and believe on them; you have to learn their strengths and weakness as well. You learn what motivates them and what dishearten them. When you are with them you might end up with some troublesome and not so useful teammates and controlling teammates but you still need to learn how to work with them and try to find your way around them without creating any dispute. And for all this you require skill that you will develop though escape room because you have to react on a whim. The best way to master is to frequently play with as many new people as possible. This way you will get to know different people and different challenges.

In life we have to learn to live with society and society come with every type of people from different background and with different personalities. We have every kind of people from freak to perfect. We need to learn how to interact with them and work with them and to make them do what is needed to be done. Does not matter if you are in a work environment or a shopping spree or even when you are looking for allies in a zombie apocalypse; you need to learn how to work as a team with your teammates and how to cooperate with them and achieve your goal.

So, escape games are the perfect way to build great teamwork. Each day people come together to work toward a common goal success whether you are a small business or a large corporation. Individual personalities with a variety of different skills are a vital piece of a puzzle; their contributions are a key to their success and yours too. For team building an escape room is an exciting way to motivate and focus their abilities. Our games are designed to be completely immersive as if the participants are in a real-life video game or movie. Within these realistic environments inhibitions disappear and an instinctive collaboration to overcome challenges begins as the clock counts down. The excitement builds and your team must band together and quickly process and evaluate a wide variety of puzzles and clues from new recruits to management trainees.

This fast-paced atmosphere offers the opportunity for your group to connect on a brand new level as they work together develop a plan and find solutions. So, not only are they bonding as a team but they are being entertained in the process, something they will remember and talk about. Leaders will emerge and a memorable cohesive experience is shared and the challenges faced head-on.

- ## **Out of comfort zone:**

In an escape room you are out of you comfort zone; you are lost. Sounds like it was in my life the same

This situation pushes you to change you way to thinking and makes you to view the things differently and sometimes to develop a new skill just to win the challenge. You may have to solve a puzzle that you have never seen before and you may have to use some things in a way that you never thing as possible. You take responsibility to succeed. is all about coming out of your comfort zone and view the things in new light. You will be beating yourself for not knowing what to do or to handle the situation and that pressure gave you no choice but to adapt in the situation and getting out it. In escape room there is limited time to learn you just have to do anyhow no matter what it takes. The faster you will learn the faster you will be able to handle real life situation because you already have been prepared for this in your escape room. The day you learn to adapt the day nothing will be ever difficult for you know how to fight; the life will be so much easier then.

- ## **Conclusion**

If you have never tired the escape room then now is the time to do it. It will be life shattering experience. The will be a new chapter of your life, but it new to be a high quality escape room as well. You will be astonished how fast your mind can work and how many solutions you can think of when in such situation. You mind will be thinking in a completely new direction. So, in order to achieve all that go to escape room with you friends, family, or your coworkers to improve yourselves. You will learn the taste of personal achievement.

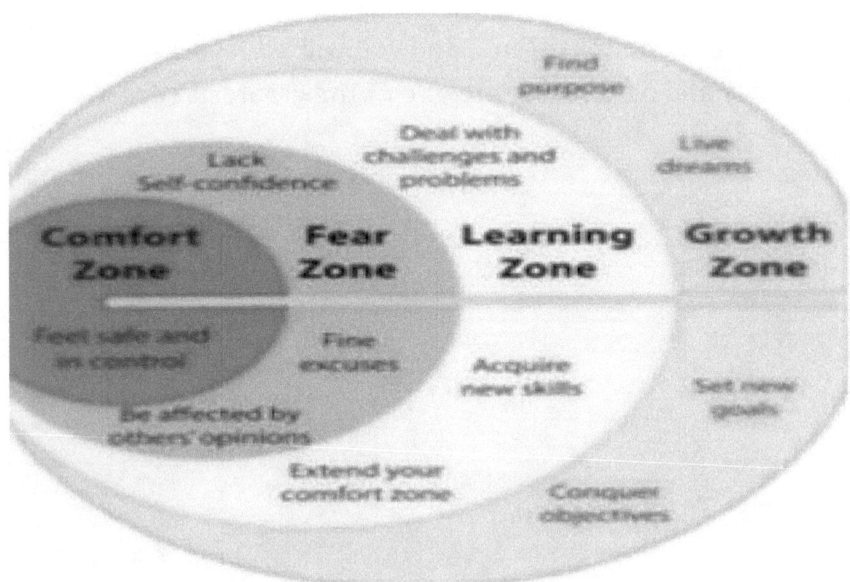

Comfort
Zone
Fear
Zone
Learning
Zone
Growth
Zone
Lack
Self-confidence
Deal with
challenges and
problems
Find
purpose
Live
dreams
Feel safe and
in control
Find
excuses
Acquire
new skills
Set new
goals
Be affected by
others' opinions
Extend your
comfort zone
Conquer
objectives

Goals

Stay consistent...be persistent...and you will achieve your goals. Consistency and persistence are two of the greatest "secrets" for success

Valorie Haugen
Executive Diamond
Direct Distributor

10 tips to succeed or what successful people do

1.Set Goals:I have never met a successful person who doesn't set goals. Without clear target to move toward a goal, you can't succeed. If you don't know where you're going, you will end up in someplace that you didn't plan to be in.Setting goals should be the number one priority for anyone seeking success.What you want -Your End Goal,make sure your "Why",your reason that you are doing what you must do is strong.When things go wrong, like they always do, you have the strength and purpose to keep going.

2. Take responsibility for your life: Another key attribute to all successful people is this: They take complete responsibility for the success and failures in their lives. If something doesn't work, they don't blame others.

They learn the lesson and move on quickly.Your thought process should be:How can I make this work?What can I learn from this?Never you live in the past or make excuses.Everyone has the opportunity to either blame others and circumstances or to focus on moving on and creating a better future.

3. Great self-discipline: Discipline is a strong trait of all successful people and this one can be developed with consistent use.

4. Be obsessed with self-development: It is human nature to want to grow and learn new things. So be open to learn new things and develop your mind through mentors, audio books and reading.

5. Successful people read a lot: That will benefit their mind and their future.

6. Manage time well:I said earlier that you can't really manage time but you can manage your events.

 Time management is essential to success. Do the most valuable task first,among the tasks that are in your list. Plan in advance - days,weeks,months before you do those things that you have in mind.Know clearly what needs to be done to complete your job and reach your goals.

7.Take risks: Often most people won't take those same risks for fear of failure.

8. Keep going even when you suffer failure and setbacks: The successful people never quit.They keep going.

9. They find a way to win: It is"the whatever it takes mentality". It is the confidence in knowing that whatever happens, I will give my all and leave nothing on the table, I will find a way to win.

10. Do what you like: Find your life's purpose.

Success is not final

failure is not fatal,

It is courage to continue that counts.

-    Winston Churchill.

Keep learning

Personally, I left school even when I had not finished year 10. My mother had an accident.In those days, it was horse accident and to keep mum's vision, doctors did many operations.

Time was ticking and we needed money.
At that time we lived in a small village. I found my first official job when I was 16 years old.It involved going to work at the farm.
I read very slowly,didn't like to read books at all but in my heart, I always dreamed to live in a big house with private beach, have a lot of beautiful trees and flowers around the house. But till 35 years old, I never saw a sea in real life, yet I kept having visions and dreams. Years went by.

Every year,I asked myself more and more questions. I asked myself why I was not successful.
What was I doing wrong? I tried my best but it still was not what I wanted. I wanted a different life.

Do you ask yourself those same questions? Great!It means that you are a forward-looking person and maybe you are happy with life but are still not satisfied.
I can share the secret on how to change this situation.The secret is in you.
Event Management
To change your life and grow,
You need to develop in specific areas of your life:

- Mental
- Emotional
- Physical
- Spiritual

Are you investing in your mind? When was the last time that you were in a self-development seminar?

How long and how often are you reading books,by *authors like Dale Carnegie, Robert Kiyosaki, Robert A. Rom* and many other great authors who through books can help change your life?

Start to dream, set goals. Take responsibility.Develop Self-discipline.

When it comes to event management, people always say that it is time management that is the problem. But we can't manage time as it is always ticking.We can manage just our events, what we are doing. We can live three days in one.

I wake up early and I start my day by reading the book *Miracle Morning.*

I split my day into three from 5 A.M. till 12 P.M., from 12 P.M. till 5 P.M.and from 5 P.M. till 10 P.M.

From 5 A.M.till 8 A.M., you have 3 hours to invest in yourself to grow emotionally,physically, spiritually and mentally.

You can do the meditation.Read the books for 15- 20 minutes.Do physical exercise.It is the productive time when you are preparing yourself not only for one day.

From 8 A.M. till 12 P.M. is a very productive time at work. After that, take a break and have some great food full of goodness and nutrition. Take some supplements and vitamins,especially plant - based. We will be back later on this in the health section. I will tell you how to improve on it and even till 5 P.M. you can stay energetic and motivated and it starts to change anything around step-by-step.From 5 P.M. till 10 P.M. is the time whence can grow and develop something more, not just watching television.

 Five years ago, our mentor Rimantas Brazdeikei told us to go for a self-development seminar.We didn't have the money so he asked that maybe we could stop watching the television and rather go for a seminar, have more positivist and more money. So, we decided to sell the Television and raise money to go for that seminar and it was the best decision and investment in our mind and future.

Five years later, it changed everything in every area of our family life.

My oldest son Yanis dreamed big, was married two years after he started Escape rooms business.He became a millionaire.Another son of mine Arnis married and I have two amazing grand-kids and have a business at Stoke on Trent. As for me, I have become an author and helping to deal with family business.So many times, I learn a lot from my youngest son Imants.He sets goals.My daughter Ellie Mai was 13years old when she started to read self development book and dreaming to have her own restaurant animation studio. She knew how her house would look like in the future.

It would never have happened if we did not change our environment, if we did not change who we were in contact with everyday. We started to read books,special books which were recommended by our friends from Amway and from Yager group education.

Every month, we kept going to those education seminars and never stopped doing that.If we want to escape from our unhappy lives, debts,negativity, etc,then we have to take different information from 5% of the population,the successful people.

You cannot win if you do not begin!

Some of you maybe thinking: "Yes, I have tried so many times to change my life but nothing happened". Did you change habits? I started my exercise but after one day, after one week, I stopped doing that. There is the most important key to succeeding. Whatever you want to change, you need to keep doing it consistently for a minimum of 90 days.

I am someone who needs to see results very quickly in the things I do. If I don't have results, I usually think that the thing is not for me.Then I came to understand that to have results,I need commitment which takes time.Let me explain.It is like the seeds of tomatoes.When you plant them, you will not see tomatoes but you can only have a mental picture of the tomatoes and then it takes time, it takes some effort.You have to look after those seeds for a long time and after four months; you can see the first fruits of tomatoes.

For me, the family is very important.

I would like to share one letter from lady Daniella Kennedy.

It is really what I feel all my life, inside my soul.

Mother to her son...

My life was not crystal stairs, there were nails on it and splinters torn off boards, there were places on the floor uncovered carpet I climbed it higher and higher.

To the landings and turns, Sometimes I made my way in complete darkness. Therefore son Don't turn back,

Don't sit on the steps.

When you realize that everything is not so simple, Do Not back down now. After all. I'm still walking along it.

My son

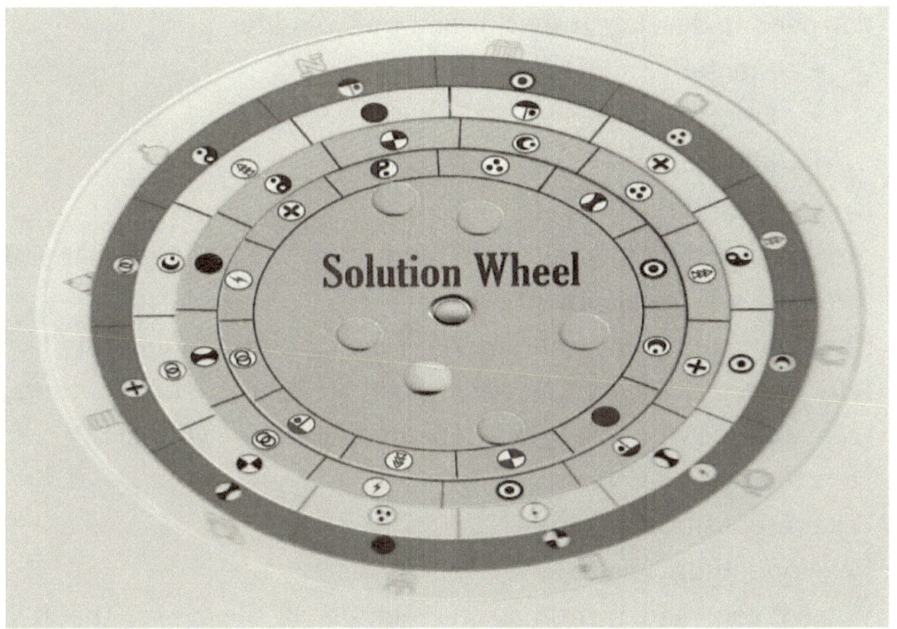

Self Discipline

To change your life and grow,
You need to develop in specific areas of your life:
- Mental
- Emotional
- Physical
- Spiritual

Are you investing in your mind? When was the last time that you were in a self-development seminar?

How long and how often are you reading books by authors like *Dale Carnegie, Robert Kiyosaki, Robert A. Rom* and many others, great authors who through books can help change your life?

Start to dream, set goals.

Take responsibility

Develop self-discipline

When it comes to event management, people always say that it is time management that is the problem. But we can't manage time as it is always ticking.We can manage just our events, what we are doing.

We can live three days in one.

I wake up early and start my day by reading the book *Miracle Morning*.

I split my day into three sections: from 5 A.M. till 8 A.M. from 8 A.M. till 5 P.M. and from 5 P.M. till 10 P.M.

From 5 A.M. till 8 A.M. you have 3 hours to invest in yourself to grow emotionally, physically, spiritually and mentally.

You can do the meditation.Read the books for 15- 20 minutes.Do physical exercise.It is the productive time when you are preparing yourself not only for one day.But the main point is that you start to build self-discipline and change habits.You have 5-8 A.M. for work on yourself,5 P.M -10 P.M. to do extra work for yourself and your family.
Are you ready to start?

DECISION

Our greatest weakness lies in giving up.
The most certain way to succeed is always to try just one more time.
- Thomas A. Edison

There are a few people who make the right decisions and there are a few people who make the wrong decisions but the majority of people really never make a decision at all. They simply complain about the results.

I decide and it is easy and quick.You make decisions everyday.You wake up early or 30 minutes before you have to run to work,drink some tea, coffee or water, watch television or read a book,buy organic food or cheap fast food. We all like to make decisions.My opinion is that we don't have bad decisions.If something is not going like you predicted or planned, take it like an experience to learn something from.

Five years ago, our mentor Rimantas Brazdeikei told us to go for a self-development seminar.We didn't have the money.So,he asked that maybe we could stop watching television.We made the decision to sell the television, raise money and go for that self - development seminar.It was easy for us but our friendliness understand why we did this. The most difficult part for people is when they make a decision and it starts at the time when you have to change yourself.You have to stay committed to what you had decided.

For us, it was simple because we were people who were forward-looking and who understood that what you're doing everyday

leads you to your goals and dreams or to the opposite direction.It
all depends on what you are doing everyday.

Dreams

First, we have to find out what dreams we have. If you don't know where you are going, how will you ever know when you get there? People who don't make a choice are no better off than people who don't have a choice.

My oldest son is a big dreamer. I call him "Yanis Dream Big". He really helps me and his two brothers to never give up but to be positive no matter what happened. Yanis is a very good example for his younger sister. He started his Escape Rooms business with a negative balance in his bank account. He created from scratch a great team,opened four venues in UK and in two years' time,he became a millionaire.

He is like a magnet for people. Everyone likes to be with Yanis but it had not always been like that. One day he will write a book and share his wisdom which will help people to change their lives.

It was his 25[th]birthday in April, 2014 when we decided to attend the self-development seminar for the first time.

What happened? Seminar?

Yes, it happened not in one day.The mindset can't be changed in one day.It takes work.The biggest work that we are supposed to do is to work on our mind-set and dreams.

Ask yourself:What dreams do I have?Many people struggle to announce their dreams.They don't have and no one asks them about dreams.

Keep The Door Open; Look For Opportunities.

Opportunities for what?

Oh, good question. Every one of us has our own dreams, hope and the desire to have the chance to achieve a better life.

All of us deserve this but it is only 15% of the population that have a life style exactly how they dreamt about.

Do you have dreams?

The biggest problem of the 21st Century is that we are so busy. We forget to stop and think. Every day, we have so many worries, afraid of what may probably never happen.

Probably because it needs a lot of courage to make this move, to seek a better life, overcome fear and such hardship these days.

I grew up in a very poor family. My dad passed away when I was 5 years old. My mom was working hard on the farm. I loved my mom and respected her for all that she has done to raise us three kids alone.

Around me were good people. Some of them were smarter than me and some of them were richer. My grades at school had not been so good.

The time came when I did two full time jobs 6 days a week. Everyday, I was always asking God to show me the way out and what I had to do differently to achieve a better life. I understood that if you went to the high school and university, working hard for 30 years, 40 years, 50 years, it is all good. But something is missing.

One day, I received a message from a stranger. Her name was Vilija.

She asked me these questions, "Do you need more money? Do you have any dreams?

At that time I had only two dreams. One was to have more money and the other was to sleep at least 6 hours a night.

I was working 16 hours a day, 6 days a week. I had four kids, I was divorced, broke, in debt of 124 000 British pounds, no free time, no money and no health.

I was ready to learn, listen and sacrifice some things.

Today, I can tell for sure that when the student is ready, the teacher appears.

So what would have happened if I did not win a million? Thanks to God, I won much more when I did join the mentorship group - these are people who have financial and personal freedom and they are helping me and other thousands of people to start our dreams and change our way of thinking.

It is very important to know what kind of people are around you, the people with whom you are connected.

During the first year, people laughed at me. But I was amazed by my mentors. They were very different people, very honest, and they helped me to become a better person than I was yesterday.

They taught me to start my dream again, love people and help them to start thinking differently.

The Mentorship Yager group helped me and others to change habits and develop an entrepreneurial mindset and know what it takes to succeed.

They impact on people and through impacting on people we make money too.

First, we need to start thinking. Then start thinking correctly, and start visualizing our dreams. When you start to think correctly, you start to take different decisions and the result of this is that you will have different results in all different areas of your life.

Commitment

Gentleman, I have a question for you: If you like a girl and you think that you should get married to this girl. Are you committed to this idea involving this girl? Should you send messages everyday or once a month?If you build your business, you should be doing 24/7 all what has to be done,whatever it takes. Then you can achieve some success not once a month for sure.

Pain

Most of the lessons I learned from my life were lessons learned through pain.

I've never known anyone who said,"I love problems".No one says that but that is the key to growth.Grow in different areas of your life.

What really helps me to handle all my pains is the Yager system education.When the people share with you their stories, you will understand that you don't have a big problem like others have. Yet, they are still fighting,still staying positive and become better persons by the day.

When my son Yanis and I attended the first self- development seminar in 2014, I was broke. I had incurred 124,000 Pounds debt. I had 4 kids-three sons who were23,22 and 18 years old and a daughter who was 5 years old. My son Imants was 18 years old playing football when he broke his leg. Doctors made so many mistakes and then they said:"You have to sign documents to cut his leg".

It was quite painful.My heart was in big pain.But with the right decision and positive vision and big help from friends,colleagues,neighbour, we were able to keep his leg and now he is walking,dancing,etc.

People like you and me have a lot of different experiences through life but it is always where you put your focus that helps you to overcome the challenges. Ask yourself: "What have I learn from this situation?Or do you just take all negativity and become more and more stressed and as a result of stress you become poor?

Pain2

Life is filled with ups and downs.The problem is that what most of us want is ups and ups. That's not possible. I think it is pretty obvious that nobody gets to escape bad experiences.

We can do everything in our power to avoid negative experiences but they have a way of finding us.Like today's situation,for example.In all parts of the world a crazy virus attacks us. How many times have you heard the expression: "Life is what we cause to happen?" Just don't stop. Stand up again and again if you get screwed up or you made some mistakes. learn from those. The more you make mistakes, the more you can learn just how to avoid the same mistakes.

It is very important to stay positive and be happy even when you have a problem.

Like I usually say, if we have a problem,it shows that we are still alive,as it is only the living that can have problems.

People who know me personally think I don't have any problems at all as I am always smiling, positive and energetic.But it had not always been like this.

You have to teach yourself how to be happy today with all the problems that you are yet having not when you win a one million lottery.

What sort of parent are you?

If you don't have kids yet, you are still viewed as a child by someone. You can see this point from different perspectives.

We have many customers who are coming with different kids. In order not to over-complicate things, they see, think and do things differently. They don't have so many restrictions in their brains like we adults have. What sort of parent are you?

What sort of parent are you? Are you the sort that is patient? Are you the sort that is wise? Or you care only about what others say?

I was running games like game master last 3 years. I saw many families with kids of different ages.

And what I realized is that we parents like to think that everything we are doing is right and our kids are supposed to listen to us. Does that sound like what you do?

I think every one of us has similar thoughts or feelings like: "I don't like what my child is saying or what they do or how they act". This is especially so when a child reaches teen age.

I would like to share an experience with you. I had the same feelings and thoughts. But then I started watching what was happening inside the room when the family was actually playing a game let's say with a 5-year- old child.

In Escape rooms games, there are no restrictions for age. We have families with babies and we have families who come with parents who are elderly.

I started to realize that the kids are much quicker to adapt to new surroundings.

I saw a child bring actual answers to the parents but they were not taking it seriously, not paying attention to that.

We do not stop and then ask the child, "What do you mean? Why are you thinking like that?We love our children, so why don't we start to respect them?

Do you pick up your child when others put him or her down, or bullying the child? At least don't do it yourself.

How many times does your stress have a negative impact on your child? When you have problems at work, relationship problems, financial problems or others in the family or what the teacher said about your child, what he has done right or done wrong, what is your own perspective?

The "What's wrong" or "what's right" perspective or how you understand it is the expectation from your own perspective.

The teacher, the school, you, everyone is locked in a CAGE of rules. We are not interested in people.

How about starting to ask questions and being prepared to listen and hear?

Our present generation is a digital time.

Many moms have problems. The kids are addicted to phones.

A mom pulls the phone out from the hand of the child and the results of that are panic and stress for both. How would you feel if someone pulled a phone out from your hand when you are in the middle of something which you believe is important?

My daughter is 14 years old now. I learn a lot from Ellie. Yes, I do. She teaches me to find in people only good things,not to pre-judge people.

We can't Judge people whose history we don't know.

Relationship

So long as we love,we serve. So long as we are loved by others, I would almost say that we are indispensable. No man is useless while he has a friend.

It is the painful part of life for the soul. I am a mum of 4 kids. Thanks to God, with all of them we have great relationships. But it had not always been like that.

For good relationship, you have to work on that. And start from yourself not from your partner,son,daughter,parents. You have to learn how to listen and respect people.It is not easy because everyone thinks he is right and from his own standpoint he is right. The book by *Dale Carnegie*is very good. It explains this.For me, it was not always easy to have contact with the C-type of people. You will ask:What is this C-type? I personally read self-help books such as 'Positive Personality Profiles' by *Robert A.Rohm.*

Many years ago, I realised how many friends I had. Friends are different.

When my son Imants had an accident, the people who knew us worked with us.They started to help us collect some money for plane and operation. Till today, we still cherish one another.

Social media are really helpful these days as you can communicate so quickly.

Some people who we thought were our friends betrayed us.

We find the best friends on our way when we start to surround ourselves with positive people.We call these people like Amway People.

The first real friends were Rimantas and Liana Brazdeikei,Saulus and Lina Shakinej

and of course Daina and Zilvinas Elvikei.I am very thankful to these people for what they have been doing in his life and share love and wisdom and also believe in one another.

Relationship requires work on yourself.It is the hardest job in our lives.Every business is successful because of people's skills.

I read Dale Carnegie's books so many times and come back again and again to those books.

It is a person's decision where to be and how to act.I heard one story about a family.The mom and dad were drinking and had two sons.One became very successful and one became an alcoholic.Ask them the same question:"Why are you so different when you had the same situation in life?" Both of them would answer:"It is because my family was drinking and I didn't have another choice".

Health, Nutrition,Food Supplements, Vitamins, Nutrients.

At age 35, I was so poorly exhausted. I visited doctors again and again with the hope that they could help me.

But my health was going worse and worse by the day.

In 2014, Rimantas Brazdeikei who later became our mentor helped a lot.He is a direct-selling business owner working with Amway. He started to ask questions:"What foods are you eating? Do you exercise? Do you know something about supplements,vitamins and minerals and do you take them?"

It takes time to change habits and our thinking before we become vegans and vegetarians,avoid using dairy products and using a lot supplements and vitamins.

They introduced Nutrilite to us.

Nutrilite is already 80 years old in the market and why does the use of Nutrilite keep growing in the market through all these years? They produce plant-based supplements.

Amway company was founded in 1959 by Richard Da Vos and Jay Van Andel.These entrepreneurs had originally started Ja-Ri Corporation in 1949, importing goods from South America to resell.

They attended Nutrilite seminar and changed Ja-Ri to a Nutrilite distributor company and managed to attract many distributors but the stability of Nutrilite gave them concerns.

So they formed The American Way-Amway to protect the distributors by finding more products than just Nutrilite. Nutrilite was founded in 1934 by C. F. Rehnborg.

In 1956, one of the first Vitamins C supplements derived from a natural source was presented.

In 2002, Nutrilite was recognised as the only global vitamins and mineral brand to grow,harvest and process plants on their own certified organic farms.

BodyKey by Nutrilite was introduced in 2013.

In more than 64 countries worldwide, people are using these amazing plant-based vitamins. In their farms they never use pesticides or herbicides or any synthetic chemicals.

Health 2

Food, genes, environment and disease
Your body is composed entirely of molecules derived from food.In a lifetime you eat 100 tons of food,which is broken down by enzyme-rich secretions in the digestive tract produced at the rate of about ten liters per day. Macro nutrients [fats, proteins, carbohydrates] and micro nutrients [vitamins, minerals] are absorbed through the digestive tract whose health and integrity depend fundamentally on what you eat. Your nutritional status determines, to a substantial extent,your capacity to adapt and maintain health.

Biochemical imbalances resulting from sub-optimum nutrition experienced over generation are recorded and expressed genetically as strengths and weaknesses of specific body processes.

Your genes express themselves in your environment [food,air,water and so on] If your environment is too hostile for them,you cannot adapt and disease results.

If your environment is nourishing,you have greater resistance to disease and are more likely to experience health and vitality.

Your health can be promoted and maintained at the highest level if you are able to achieve your optimal intake of each nutrient every single day.

Gradually, your entire body,including your skeleton is rebuilt and rejuvenated.

Through optimum nutrition you can;

- Improve mental clarity,mood and concentration
- Increase IQ
- Increase physical performance
- Improve the quality of sleep
- Improve resistance to infections
- Protect yourself from disease
- Extend your healthy lifespan

Health 3

Here are few simple tips to help you conform to your natural design:

- Get up earlier in summer and later in winter,in natural sunlight hours. Don't eat late at night,
before you are fully awake.
- Eat when you are hungry not out of habit.Eat little and often,with plenty of fruits as snacks in between.
- Eat food as raw and unprocessed as possible. Avoid synthetic chemicals.
- Avoid concentrated foods such as sugar or sweeteners.Dilute fruit juices.Drink plenty of water.
- Minimize your intake of dairy foods,refined wheat and grains.
- Take frequent exercise and keep active.
- Eat mainly vegan diet,with half your intake of food consisting of fruits,vegetables,seed sprouts,nuts,seeds. If you do eat meat, avoid the intensively-reared kind.Choose fish or organic-made instead. Eat these foods only with vegetables.

Make sure your organisms have plenty of supplements and vitamins:

-Vitamin C

-Vitamin group B,Omega 3

-Multi - vitamins and minerals. You can always find plant-based vitamins at the link below to build your health.

Spring water treatment system is available too but people don't know about it and are still buying plastic bottles

http://www.amway.co.uk/user/serafima123

Mind set

The biggest lesson I have ever learned is the stupendous importance of what we think.

If I knew what you think,I would know what you are,for your thoughts make you what you are. By changing our thoughts,we can change our lives.

I once heard that you can't solve today's problems with yesterday's solutions. It is so true.We have to learn and grow a bit more to find the solutions.

Mindfulness is the process of actively noticing new things.When you do that,it puts you in the present.It makes you more sensitive to context and perspective.

Mindfulness helps you to appreciate why people behave the way they do.It made sense to them at the time or else they wouldn't do it.

Mindfulness helps us realize that there are no positive or negative outcome. There is A,B,C,D,E or more, each with its challenges and opportunities. Let me explain.

There's an old story about two people coming before a Judge.One guy tells his side of the story and the Judge says, "That's right".

The other guy tells his side of the story and the Judge says,"That's right".

They said,"We can't be both right" and the Judge says,"That's right".

Instead of letting people lock into their positions,go back and open it up.Then find a way for both of them to be right.

I realised our life is the reflection of our self–talk.

What we are constantly saying to ourselves is what becomes our reality.

Five years ago, my health was not in the best condition and I started to change the way of thinking and I started seeing things differently too.It took time.

Now, my health is much better than it was five years ago.

let me explain.

If you keep saying that you are forgetful,you are talking yourself into forgetting.If you tell yourself that you are wise and healthy,you'll tend toward that as your reality.

You need to start thinking since your words are creative by nature.

Then start to take different actions.

SUCCESS

Success - It has to do with making wise decisions.

Any success, small or big, starts from making a decision.
We cannot grow if we let others make decisions for us.There is one proven way not to grow and not to develop.This is not determination.
You cannot make a decision? Then, someone will make it for you.
Let's say you are in the escape room with a team.It is fine if someone makes a decision.Maybe it helps or not but no matter what, do not always allow someone to make decisions for you.

Success is the decision you make today.Exactly today!
Tomorrow is not here yet. Yesterday is past and it is never going to be back.We have only today and now.
Check yourself and ask simple questions:"What I'm doing now in every twenty minutes, is it going to help me to achieve my dreams and goals?"Remember, success is a journey.
Many are afraid what others will say.Sometime ago, I had a different mindset. I was always thinking and I was concerned about what others said. My mentor asked me a question: "Do other people pay your debts and bills? Are they really interested in your success and financial success?Find a person,a business or workplace where your mentor will be interested to help you grow.
Wealth - It is how much we have a free time to enjoy life with our close friends and family.
Do You have finances which are coming in passively and do you have freedom of choice?

47

Start today to change little things, start from yourself.
The Success in You

The answers to life's questions are within you; You just need to look, to listen and believe!

LIST OF RECOMMENDED BOOKS

Dale Carnegie-How to challenge yourself and others to Greatness
Patrick Alford- The Optimum Nutrition Bible
Napoleon Hill - Think and Grow Rich
David J.Schwartz, P.D - The Magic of Thinking Big
Dexter Yeager- The Pursuit
Gary Chapman -The 5 Love of Languages
Dr.John Martini - The values Factor